Ideas on How To

Talk to the "Boss"

Read and Study the Bible for Yourself,

Intentionally and Like It

By Cynthia Radtke

First edition

This book was professionally typeset on Reedsy.

Find out more at reedsy.com

2

This book is dedicated to my mother, Marilou, for establishing an extraordinary example of someone who daily walks with the Lord. Her commitment to teach me how to study God's word has been the most rewarding and beneficial endeavor in my life!

I also want to recognize Beachy from The Firs Bible Camp in Bellingham, WA for reinforcing a daily commitment to Bible reading and an author named, Ann Kiemel Anderson, who wrote about her experiences sharing God in her daily life.

...the mind governed by the Spirit of God is life and peace.

Romans 8:6

Table of Contents

Introduction & Purpose

Welcome to my experiences in spending time communicating with God. In the next few pages, you will read some ideas on how to talk to our Boss, Jesus, our Lord and Savior.

There are two reasons for writing this book. First, it is a passion of mine to see others grow in their relationship with Jesus, and to have a deep understanding of who He is and how much He loves us! Second, many people have asked for ideas of how to study the Bible and grow in their knowledge of God. So, in the following pages, you will read about different methods I have used for studying the Bible.

As a suggestion, use a technique for a month or so until you feel confident. After that, switch it up and try another one.

I am always looking for other suggestions or ways to study God's word. Feel free to share some of your ideas with me at

howtotalktotheboss@gmail.com.

Prologue

Spending time with God means getting to know Him. The Bible is His written word and for those who know Him personally, it is our lifeline.

If you aren't familiar with Him individually yet, know this: He loves you and offers freedom from all wrongdoings. In the Bible, it tells us in Romans 3:23, that all have sinned, and no one is innocent.

Through His death and resurrection, He offers deliverance from our sin and eternal life. In Romans 6:23, it reminds us that sin leads to death, but that God's gift is eternal life through His son, Jesus.

By offering us the gift of salvation, He has established an opportunity for a relationship with us. We only need to accept this as payment for the things we have done wrong. Romans 10:13 tells us that ALL who call on the name of the Lord will be saved.

As a result of accepting this gift from God, we have a wonderful message of hope. In Romans 5:1 we hear that we are now clean and have peace with God because of Jesus' death and resurrection.

If you have not received God's gift of eternal life, I hope you will consider praying and asking Jesus to forgive you and be in control of your life.

It is as simple as saying, "Jesus, please forgive me for the things I have done wrong. Thank you for covering my sins on the cross and for your forgiveness! Change my life and give me your peace as I want to live for You."

If you have chosen to accept His gift,
then this book is the next step in getting
to know God.

I wish you closeness and growth in your pursuit

of knowing Jesus our Savior!

Thanks for seeking God.... here we go!

Materials & Prayer Preparation

Suggested List of Materials

- Journals
- Writing utensils - colors are great
- Various versions of the Bible
- Concordances
- Bible Commentary
- World Maps
- Devotionals
- Dictionary
- 3 x 5 Cards

Prayer Preparation

Start your time reflecting in prayer:

→ Confession (naming your sin before God)

→ Acknowledge who God is (Numbers 23:19, Deuteronomy 32:4, Ephesians 3:12)

→ Put on the Armor of God (Ephesians 6:10-18)

→ Claim verses for your time with Him (Psalms 119:18; Psalms 119:130-135; Ephesians 3:20 & 11 Corinthians 9:8)

→ Pray for domestic and international issues. Suggested resources:

- Christianheadlines.com

- Alliance Defending Freedom - adflegal.org

- American Center for Law and Justice - aclj.org

- Christianpost.com

- Voice of Martyrs - persecution.com

Pray for others. Keep a list of people and rotate through it. Pray for about five people a day and see how God connects you with updates for those on your prayer list.

Time to Talk to the Boss!

Idea #1

Check Up, Thx and Commit to God
(Credit to my mom, Marilou Mae!)

Check Up   Thank you so much! Thx   Commit to God

<u>Action Steps</u>

1. In your journal, make three columns titled:
   Check Up, Thx and Commit to God.

2. Under the "Check Up" write down things
   you need to confess. This could include
   negative attitudes, behaviors, lack of
   control, negative thoughts or actions.

3. Under the "Thx" column, write things
   from a grateful and appreciative heart.

4. Under the "Commit to God" column, write down concerns, goals, frustrations, and hopes.

5. Once complete, take some time to reflect and pray about each category.

For example:

<u>Confession</u>

"Jesus, I confess to you my struggle with my co-worker and my negative attitude. Help me see her through your eyes and love her with your love."

<u>Thx</u>

"Father, thank you so much for the sun peeking through the clouds this morning. It is refreshing. Also, thank you for my spouse who is a HUGE support in my life."

<u>Commit to God</u>

"God, I have so many plans and such a busy day. It is hard for me to see it all get accomplished. So, here is my list of things for today that need to get done: cleaning, planning the June trip, birthday presents for May, dinner, my college classes and two doctor appointments. I leave these tasks at your feet and commit my day to you. Let me hear your direction and thank you."

<u>Application</u>

1. Pray these verses below to yourself. These focus on committing your day to God and that is exactly what He wants us to do!

   Proverbs 16:3 (AMP) "Roll your works upon the Lord, commit and trust them to Him; He will cause your thoughts to be agreeable to His will and your plans will be established and succeed."

Psalms 32:8 (NIV)

"I will instruct you and teach you in the way you should go; I will counsel you with My eye upon you."

Philippians 4:13 (AMP) "I can do all things [which He has called me to do] through Him who strengthens *and* empowers me [to fulfill His purpose—I am self-sufficient in Christ's sufficiency; I am ready for anything and equal to anything through Him who infuses me with inner strength and confident peace.] I can do all this through Him who gives me strength."

2. <u>Suggestion</u>: write out one verse and put it somewhere in your home where you will see it regularly. Read it frequently and God's word will calm you and give you rest.

Idea #2

Who, What, When, Where, Why & How

wwwww & H

<u>Action Steps</u>

1. From a book of the Bible, pick a verse or a section of verses to study. As you read them, answer the who, what, when, where, why and how questions and write the answers down in your journal.

For example:

Psalms 1:2-3 (NIV)

"Blessed is the one whose....delight is in the law of the Lord, and who meditates on His law day and night. That person is like a tree planted by streams of water, which yields its fruit in season and whose leaf does not wither - whatever they do prospers."

2. <u>Who is this verse talking to?</u> "the one whose delight is in the Law of the Lord". The one who enjoys reading God's word.

3. <u>What are these verses saying will happen</u>? A person who meditates and delights in God's word will be like a tree that is planted by water, bearing fruit and having no leaves that wither, they will prosper. They will be blessed.

4. <u>When is this going to happen</u>? Whenever someone "delights in His law and

meditates on it." This is a promise in the Bible and God tells us to hold Him to His promises, so claim it and meditate on His word.

5. <u>Where will this happen</u>? This will take place in "our lives or in daily living."

6. <u>Why will this happen</u>? Because this is a promise in His word. If we meditate and delight in His teaching, then we will bear fruit and not shy away from difficult situations.

7. <u>How is this going to take place</u>? God will bless us. "Blessed is the one...., you are like a tree planted by streams of living water...." We rely on His promises.

Application

1. Pray and ask God to increase your "delight" for His word and determine now to increase your time in His word, memorizing, meditating and praying.

2. Write down a new goal specifically from the verse(s) you chose to study.

Idea #3

Pick a Topic

Action Steps

1. This method consists of you choosing a topic, any topic. ......let's pick "fear."

2. Using a dictionary, look up the definition of your topic and write it in our own words in your journal.

   Fear: an unpleasant emotion from danger or anxiousness

3. Ask yourself some personal questions regarding the topic and answer them in your journal:

   ➢ What am I afraid of?

   ➢ What causes this fear?

➢ What is the worst thing that could happen?

➢ What do you do about it when it sneaks up on you?

4. Using a concordance, look up a few verses about your topic (fear) and write them out in your journal, (the whole verse).

For example: (NIV))

Psalms 27:1 "The Lord is my light and my salvation; whom shall, I fear? The lord is the stronghold of my life: of whom shall I be afraid?"

Psalms 46:1-3 "God is our refuge and strength, a very present help in trouble. Therefore, we will not fear though the earth give way, though the mountains be moved into the heart of the sea, though

the waters roar and foam, though the

mountains tremble at its swelling."

Luke 14:27 "Peace I leave with you; My

peace I give to you. Not as the world

gives do I give to you. Let not your

hearts be troubled, neither let them be

afraid."

11 Timothy 1:7 "For God gave us a spirit

not of fear but of power and love and self-

control."

Application

1. Underline one phrase that stands out to

    you from each verse.

2. Write down common promises from these verses.

3. Now, rewrite these verses and intertwine them together in your own words. Draw strength from these promises and commands from God.

4. <u>Answer the question</u>: Now what does this mean in my life?

5. Pray for God to strengthen you in the area of your topic (fear).

6. Now pick one of the verses and write it on a 3x5 card and post it on your mirror.

7. Read it each morning as a promise from God to you!

   Great way to start your day!

Idea #4

Use a Devotional Book

There are so many refreshing and challenging devotionals to use during your daily time with God.

Here are a few that have been especially rewarding:

- ➢ My Utmost for His Highest by Oswald Chambers

- ➢ Streams in the Desert by L. B. Cowman

- ➢ Jesus Calling by Sarah Young

- ➢ God's Purpose for Your Life by Charles Stanley

- ➢ Our Daily Bread Ministries

➢ <u>Good Morning Lord, Can We Talk?</u> by Charles Swindoll

Action Steps

1. If you do not have one, buy one from the list or download free ones from a phone app.

   Devotionals can be organized in many ways, calendar dates, day by day, some have questions, some are topical with matching verses, some are motivational and some tell a story.

2. Once you have chosen one, open it to your starting point and begin reading.

Application

1. After completing the daily devotional, get your journal out and reflect on what was said to you. What stood out? Were there words of scripture that encouraged you? Was there a phrase from the reading that motivated or convicted your heart?

2. Write your answers in your journal.

3. Pray and thank God for His teaching.

4. Set goals for yourself for daily application from the reading.

"The great word of Jesus to His disciples is 'abandon'. When God has brought us into the relationship of disciples, we have to venture on His word; trust entirely on Him and watch that when He brings us to the venture, we take it."

Studies on the Sermon on the Mount
by Oswald Chambers

Idea #5

Use a Variety of Bible Versions

This method will have you using multiple Bibles. You will be comparing scripture verses using each version and digging deeper into the meaning of the Word of God.

<u>Action Steps</u>

1. Pick three different types of versions of the Bible.

For example: New International Version, New King James, the Living Bible, The Amplified Bible, New American Standard, etc.

2. Choose a specific section of the Bible to read. It can be one verse, a few verses or a whole chapter.

3. Read the section in each version one at a time. Summarize what you read for each version in your journal. This will take some time but will allow you to delve into the Bible. <u>Leave some space after each scripture section you summarized so you have additional room for more thoughts.</u>

4. Once you have read your section in each Bible version, go back and examine the words you wrote. Look for synonyms or phrases that explain the verses in a clearer way.

<u>Application</u>

1. Highlight scripture sections that were similar.

2. Underline a part that "popped out to you" and write out your thoughts about that section.

3. Write a letter to God thanking Him for what He just taught you about Himself.

4. Pray and ask Him for help in obeying what He has taught you.

<u>Here is a great resource for different types of Bible versions</u>: bibleanswers.study

Idea #6

Word by Word Verse Study

This is a focus on ONE verse in the Bible.

Action Steps

1. Pick a verse from the Bible. Maybe as you are reading a particular section, one verse stands out, use that one.

2. In your journal write the verse out exactly as it is in the Bible.

Fact: In the King James Bible there are 783,137 written words!
https://wordcounter

3. Now rewrite it again, but in your own words making sure you understand it.

4. In your journal, take each word from the verse and list them one at a time on their own lines.

5. Using a dictionary, write out the definition of each, (no saying you already know the meaning, just do it).

6. Look back at each word and reread what you wrote.

Fact: Did you know that the most commonly used word in the bible is "Lord". Depending on the version, it is used between 7,000 - 8,000 times.
https://thebibleanswer.org

7. Rewrite the verse again incorporating a few synonyms or phrases you found from the dictionary.

8. Look at how the verse has developed.

Application

1. Write out this verse using your name in it. What is God telling you?

2. How will you apply this promise in your daily life today?

3. Write it on a 3x5 card and commit it to memory.

Memorization Tips: put it on your home screen on your phone, post it on your mirror or fridge.

Idea #7

Letter to God

Action Steps

1. Start out writing a letter to God. Here

   are some ideas to talk with Him about:

   - Daily goals
   - To do lists
   - Tests at school
   - Work responsibilities
   - Attitude towards a person
   - Not feeling well
   - Discouragement
   - Fear of something happening that day
   - Excitement of upcoming events

Just write to Him as if He was sitting right

next to you, having a conversation. Chat about

what is on your mind.

For example:

"Good morning God -

New job today. I am a bit nervous but excited to start this new venture in my life. I am a bit concerned about tackling this with my responsibilities at home but will have to adjust and learn as I go. Help my family to have a safe and fabulous day...., etc."

**This is just a sample...but gab away.
He wants to hear your mind,
heart and soul.**

2. When you feel like you are done sharing with Him, take a verse that you know and write it in your own words to end the letter. See how you can claim His promises from the verse in your day.

A verse that I like to do this with is

Ephesians 3:20 (AMP) "Now to Him who is

able to [carry out His purpose and] do

superabundantly more than all that we dare

ask or think [infinitely beyond our greatest

prayers, hopes, or dreams], according to His

power that is at work within us."

You can hear the Amplified Version of the bible in that verse!

Application

1. Pray and thank God for listening.

2. Thank the Lord for His promises in the

   verse you wrote.

3. Start your day being refreshed or go to

   sleep now comforted by His word.

Idea #8

Reading a Proverb a Day

Action Steps

1. There are 31 chapters in the book of Proverbs. Read one chapter each day for the month.

2. Read through the whole chapter first without stopping.

3. Read it **again** slower allowing God to speak to you. He will "pop" something out to you.

4. Write out in your journal, which verses, or topics stand out.

5. Paraphrase parts of the verses and put together a poem of sorts.

6. Reread what you wrote.

<u>Application</u>

1. Share your poem with a friend to encourage them! It's God's word so how could it not!

2. Use a 3x5 card and write out in different colors three of the key points that are "take aways" for you.

3. Hang this up somewhere you will see it for encouragement.

> *God has not called you to just survive in this life - He has called you to be a wonder to your generation. Jesus has called you to live abundantly through Him - to enjoy His victory, no matter what your outward circumstances are and to be a witness of His power to all whom you meet. He wants you so <u>intertwined with Him</u> that when people look at you, they acknowledge that God is alive in you!*
>
> written by Carter Conlon

Idea #9

Psalms - Paraphrase each Verse

Action Steps

1. Start in the Psalms and read one entire chapter.

2. In your journal list the chapter's theme or themes.

3. Now, take one verse at a time and paraphrase each verse in your own words. If the chapter is long, then break it into sections. Do one section a day until you complete the chapter.

For example:

<u>Psalm 119:1 (NIV) says</u>: "Blessed are those whose ways are blameless, who walk according to the law of the Lord."

<u>My own words</u>: We are blessed in all we do as we choose to live without fault and as we obey what the word of the Lord says.

4. It might help to look up some of the words in the verses for clarity or additional meanings.

5. When you are finished, choose a writing tool with color and mark themes that are  the same in multiple verses.

6. List out the consistent themes. Are there any that connect with you in your current situation in life?

<u>Application</u>

1. Choose one theme to focus on today.

2. Ask God to give you an opportunity this week to implement this theme and watch Him do it!

Idea #10

Theme Study

Action Steps

1. There are many different types of themes in the Bible. Do a search and pick one that is of interest to you.

2. In your journal, <u>write out your own definition of that theme</u>. Do this BEFORE you do your study.

3. Using your concordance, look up <u>three to five</u> different locations of this theme throughout the Bible.

4. Write the scripture locations down in your journal.

5. Before you read these additional scriptures, ask God to give you understanding as you study and the "know how" to apply it to your life each day this week.

6. Now, choose one of the scriptures you wrote down and read that passage in the Bible.

7. After you are done, summarize the section in your own words.

8. Mark with color a few key words that emphasize the theme.

9. Do this for each Bible passage you wrote down.

10. When you have completed your list, compare your theme definition to

scripture's definition (the words you

marked in color). Write out any differences

or similarities. Use some color for

similarities and differences if you want.

THEMES IN THE BIBLE

- God rewarding faith & obedience
- love
- creation
- fruit of the spirit
- holiness
- sin & consequences
- Jesus Christ, God's Son

Application

1. Why does understanding this theme

   matter to you in your life?

2. Write the answer in your journal.

> This method can be used for a
> few days in a row. If you identified
> five different passages in the Bible
> for this theme, then read one
> passage each day.

Idea #11

Verse & Topic Study

<u>Action Steps</u>

1. Pick a topic that is of interest to you, maybe one you have been wanting to study or maybe one that you want to develop personally in your life.

2. Use a concordance, either from your Bible or a separate book and <u>look up two to four verses</u> on that topic.

3. In your journal, write out each verse in your own words.

4. Using a color, circle similarities in each verse.

5. Think about what stands out to you. Specifically, what is God talking to you about?

<u>Application</u>

1. List out a goal from studying these verses and tell yourself how you will apply it today in your life interactions. Be prepared and watch as God gives you opportunities to do this.

2. Later in the evening, come back to your journal and write out what occurred.

"Young Adults Who Read the Bible Regularly Are Far Less Stressed."
August 11, 2022, ChristianHeadlines.com

Idea #12

Bible Chapter Potpourri

Action Steps

1. Cut up a 3 x 5 card into ten strips of paper.

2. On each strip of paper, write out different chapters in the Bible.

3. Fold it in half and put it in a container.

4. Each day draw out one piece of paper and whichever chapter you choose is the one to study.

5. Before you start the chapter, read the introduction of the book that the chapter is from for historical information and cultural background.

6. Now start reading the chapter. Just read and allow God to talk to you as you go through it. Keep reading until God has something pop out at you. You might need to read it a few times.

7. When something does "pop," journal about it.

8. Write down the specific verse.

9. Put it in your own words.

10. What do you hear from the Lord?

11. You might hear more than one thing from the Lord within the chapter, so jot them all down.

<u>Application</u>

1. Based on what you have written and learned, what are you to change, or what are you to do today in relation to it?

2. Ask God to open your eyes to opportunities around you today and to apply this truth. He will give you occasions to implement this principle, so go out in faith and have fun!

This strategy can be done using a variety of methods: a book of the Bible, an individual verse, a theme, people from the Bible, etc.

Idea #13

SWORD Method

I am going to share something called the SWORD method. This method came from a source called <u>The Pursuit Bible, 11 Ways to Study the Bible</u> by David Kim. (<u>https://pursuitbible.com/ways-to-study-the-bible/</u>) Here is his direction for studying the Bible using the SWORD method according to the website above:

"The blade of the sword points upward *toward heaven*, so you ask "what do I learn about God in this passage?" Next, **the handle of the sword points down** *toward man*, so ask "what do I learn about people in this passage?" The 3rd question asks **how we apply what we learned**: "What does God want me to do?"

<u>Action Steps</u>

1. Pick a specific section from the Bible and read it.

2. Using the questions from the SWORD method, read through it again, slowly and answer the questions below in your journal.

➤ **"What does this passage teach me about God**, Jesus or the Holy Spirit?

➤ **What do I learn about mankind** in general – How and why do people act, think, and feel the way they do?

➤ What do I learn about myself personally and why I act, think, and feel the way I do? Do I identify with anyone in the story and why?" (Pursuit Bible)

Application

1. "Is there anything that God wants me to do according to this passage? Is there a **Sin to avoid**? Is there a **Promise to claim**? Is there an **Example to follow**? Is there a **Command to obey**?" (Pursuit Bible)

2. Take time to answer each of these and pray about how to achieve each.

Idea #14

Person, Place or Thing
(Credit to my mom, Marilou Mae!)

<u>Action Steps</u>

1. Choose a section of the Bible to read, whether it is one verse, one chapter or just a group of verses.

2. In your journal, ask yourself about the people, the places and the things that are happening. Answer the questions below:

<u>Person</u>

> Who are the people? What are their names, ages, positions?

- ➢ What is their relevance in the passage?
- ➢ Describe the culture they live in.
- ➢ What are they specifically doing in this passage? What is the purpose of their task?

Place

- ➢ Where does this passage take place? What is the specific setting, be descriptive in your answer.
- ➢ What is the country, the city, is it outside or inside a structure?
- ➢ Is it near a specific landmark? Use a map if necessary to deepen your understanding.

<u>Thing</u>

> What things are pertinent to the story? How are they connected to one another or the purpose of the text?

> What lesson is being taught?

> What is the focus?

> What action is taking place?

<u>Application</u>

1. Were these people from this passage obedient to God in their actions? Put yourself in a similar, yet current situation. How would you react?

2. Consider the location of the story. Have you been somewhere similar? If you have,

remember your experience, write about the details. If not, what would be of interest to you in that environment?

3. What lessons do you connect to from the events that took place in that particular passage?

Idea #15

Read an Author

This strategy incorporates using an author who writes about principles taught in the Bible.

Choose a book from an author you respect or use one from the list below.

<u>Here are some recommendations:</u>

- ➤ Charles Swindoll
- ➤ Christine Caine
- ➤ Vernon Magee
- ➤ Jan Markell
- ➤ David Jeremiah
- ➤ Billy Crone
- ➤ Jack Hibbs
- ➤ Amir Tsarfati
- ➤ Priscilla Shirer
- ➤ Charles Stanley
- ➤ Carter Conlon
- ➤ Sarah Young
- ➤ A.W Tozier
- ➤ David Wilkerson

Study books can be thematic, narrative or

specifically books about the Bible.

> The thing that approaches
> the very limits of His power
> is the very thing we as
> disciples of Jesus ought to
> believe He will do.
>
> MY UTMOST FOR HIS HIGHEST
> BY OSWALD CHAMBERS

Action Steps

1. Start reading chapter one in the book and mark areas of interest or challenge points to you.

2. When you complete the chapter, take out your journal.

3. Write down the key thoughts or ideas that stood out to you.

4. Look up the scripture used in the book for yourself and reread the indicated passages in the Bible.

Application

1. How does this author challenge you to apply what he wrote into your personal life?

2. How does it match God's word?

3. What steps do you need to take to achieve the goal from question #1?

Idea #16

Verse & Phrase Comparisons
(Modified from Cheryl Kay Dodson)

This is one of my favs!

Action Steps

1. Pick a book of the Bible you want to read.

2. Read the introduction of that book in your Bible or a concordance to give you an accurate cultural and historical perspective.

3. Start with chapter one and read one paragraph. (This might be just one, two or a few verses.)

    or

Read chapter one and when the subject material starts to change, stop. The goal is to stop reading when a new "topic" appears in your reading. Focus on the verses only related to that one specific subject.

4. In your journal, rewrite the verses you just read separating out each verse.

5. Use your Bible references to look up other verses that reinforce the topic of that particular verse.

   (Bible references can be things like the concordance, side panel explanations, numbers listed next to the verses to look up in the back of your Bible, etc.)

6. <u>Look up these verses in the Bible and write one or two next to the original verse.</u>

<u>Here is an example:</u>

Here is a passage written out, each verse separated from the next.

<u>James 1:2-4 (NIV)</u>

vs. 2 - "Consider it pure joy my brothers whenever you face trials of many kinds,

vs. 3 - because you know that the testing of your faith develops perseverance.

vs. 4 - Perseverance must finish its work so that you may be mature and complete, not lacking anything."

Using references from the Bible, here are some reinforcing biblical comparisons:

vs. 2 *"Consider it pure joy my brothers whenever you face trials of many kinds,"*

& 1 Peter 2:19 (NIV) - *"It is commendable if someone bears up under the pain of unjust suffering because they are conscious of God."*

Now, reread each of the verses you wrote down and write the promises from both verses.

James 1:2 & 1 Peter 2:19

> We are to consider it joy and also commendable if we stay joyful in our trials, because it will make us conscious of God. We will have a greater awareness of God during unfair suffering. Many people turn

to God when they go through difficult
times.

Next verse:

vs. 3 "Because you know that the testing of
your faith develops perseverance."

& Job 17:9 (NIV) - "Nevertheless, the righteous
will hold to their ways, and those with clean
hands will grow stronger."

Again, reread each of the verses you wrote down
and write the promises from both verses.
James 1:3 & Job 17:9

> The testing of our faith will help us
> develop perseverance in our struggles as
> we trust in the Lord to help us get

through it. We are promised that we can hold to doing what is right and as we do this, we will grow stronger in persevering.

Last verse:

vs. 4 "Perseverance must finish its work so that you may be mature and complete, not lacking anything."

& Hebrews 12:1 (NIV) - "Therefore since we are surrounded by such a great cloud of witnesses, let us throw off everything that hinders and the sin that so easily entangles. And let us run with perseverance the race marked out for us."

Again, reread each of the verses you wrote down and write the promises from both verses.

James 1:4 & Hebrews 12:1.

> We must complete the work God has for
> us no matter what we are facing. This
> will increase our spiritual maturity and
> help us be confident in knowing we lack
> nothing as we trust in the Lord for our
> circumstances. We also must be ready to
> throw off any temptation that Satan will
> throw at us. Sin can tangle us up and we
> need to be strong and stay focused on
> God.

Application

1. Reread and meditate on God's promises in
each section.

2. Thank God for opening your mind up to a deeper understanding of how the Bible reinforces its truth, scripture by scripture.

Idea #17

Book of the Bible

Action Steps

1. Choose a book to read from the Bible.

2. Start reading from the introduction to gain a cultural and historical perspective.

3. Search up a timeline and/or map of this book if one is not provided in your Bible.

4. In your journal, write out some categories for keeping track of information.

   Categories like the:

   - Characters
   - Themes
   - Truths
   - Historical Relevance

5. Read an entire chapter with no interruption. Relax and enjoy this time with the Lord.

6. Now, go back and reread the same passage and fill in details after each of the categories you chose to study.

Application

1. What parallels do you find in your current life?

2. How does/can this passage of scripture affect your life today?

Idea #18

Characters in the Bible

Action Steps

1. Choose a character from the Bible.

Some examples:

Paul	Hannah
Samson	Elisha
Jesus	Esther
David	

2. Using your biblical references, find two or three areas in the Bible where this character is discussed.

3. Write these scripture references down in your journal.

4. Depending on your time, read all of them or a few each day.

5. Answer these questions about the character:

   ➤ What positive impact did they leave on people around them and why?

   ➤ Was there a specific request they had from God? If so, what happened?

   ➤ How was their heart towards the Lord?

Application

1. How would you respond to God in a similar situation?

2. What impact would this person have in your current environment?

3. What impact would this character have in the world you now live?

4. What example does this person set for us as believers of Jesus? How should you apply this to your current life?

Scientific Facts Found in the Bible

- The earth is round - Isaiah 40:21-22
- All languages have the same origin - Genesis 11:6-9
- Air has weight - Job 28:25
- Eagles have telescopic eyes - Job 39:26-29

New International Bible (NIV)

Idea #19

Bible App + Scripture

Action Steps

1. Choose a Bible app that has a "verse a day" to download on your phone. It usually will notify you each day to read that verse.

2. If you don't have one, here are some suggestions:

   - OnePlace

   - The Daily Bible

   - World Challenge

   - Behold Israel

   - Voice of Martyrs

   - Real Life with Jack Hibbs

3. Each day, read the verse from the app you chose.

4. Then, using your Bible, open to the same chapter and verse. Take time to read the entire chapter to put that verse into context.

5. Write down some broad thoughts on what you have learned.

6. Now, go back to the original specific verse. Reread it and write down what God is talking to you about in that particular verse. If you need to, write it out and put it in your own words.

7. Some of the Bible apps also have daily devotionals; choose one and take some

time and read that day's additional message.

8. In your journal write down what the devotional is teaching you.

Application

1. What is the main point of the verse and what is it telling you today?

2. How will you prepare to follow the guidance from this verse?

3. How will you take steps today to implement the devotional's objective?

4. Pray and ask God to help you change anything He has shown you from His word.

Idea #20

Reading Through a Commentary

Love this one!
This method is like being taught in a Bible class!

Action Steps

1. Choose a book of the Bible and read the first chapter.

2. Summarize the chapter in your journal.

3. Choose a commentary with that particular book of the Bible.

4. Now, read the same chapter in the commentary.

5. Write down additional lessons shared by the author of the commentary that stood out to you.

6. What differences do you see from your perspective versus the author of the commentary?

Recommended commentary authors:
➤ J. Vernon McGee
➤ Charles Swindoll
➤ David Jeremiah
➤ C.S. Lewis
➤ Hank Hanegraaff
➤ Ken Ham

Application

1. What insights did you receive from reading the commentary's perspective?

2. What particular verses were emphasized with longer explanations? Why do you suppose?

3. How is this relevant to you today?

4. Take time to pray for this author or thank the Lord for his/her ministry.

Conclusion

There you have it. Twenty strategies for digging into God's word.

This book is all about spending time with our Savior, our Boss, Jesus Christ. Determine to schedule out a time each day.

Treat this time as priority #1!

It won't be easy, there are always distractions, legitimate distractions. But, remember, your child, your "to do list", your animals, your friend who needs you and your spouse are loved and cared for MORE by our Boss than we could ever imagine!

These ideas are meant to inspire,

challenge and encourage you to grow deeper in

your relationship in knowing Jesus!

My prayer is that you "take off" and sense the

need of seeing Jesus in the Word of God and grow

more like Him!

I would love to hear back from you with some of your ideas. If you wish to share any of them, just email me at howtotalktotheboss@gmail.com. Perhaps in the next volume, I will have opportunity to include your suggestion.

If you have received any value from this book, I would appreciate a favorable review for the book on Amazon.

Resources

Chambers, O. (1960). *Studies in the Sermon on the Mount* (4th ed.). London ; Marshall Morgan & Scott.

Conlon, C. (2018). *It's Time to Pray.* GPC Books, a division of Times Square Church, in partnership with Charisma House.

Dexter, A. (n.d.). *Wordcounter.io.* Wordcounter.Io. Retrieved August 31, 2022, from https://wordcounter.io/blog/how-many-words-are-in-the-bible

Foust, M. (2022, November 8). *Christian Headlines.* Https://www.Christianheadlines.Com. Retrieved August 31, 2022, from https://www.christianheadlines.com/blog/young-adults-who-read-the-bible-regularly-are-far-less-stressed-new-report-finds.html

Kim, D. (n.d.). *Pursuit Bible*.
Https://Pursuitbible.Com/Ways-to-Study-the-Bible/.
Retrieved August 31, 2022, from
https://pursuitbible.com/ways-to-study-the-bible/

Thompson, D.D., Ph. D., F. C. (1978). *Thompsons Chain
Reference Bible, New International Version*. The B.B.
Kirkbride Bible Company, Inc. and Zondervan Corporation.

United Church of God, Australia. (n.d.). *Bible Answers*.
Https://Bibleanswers.Study/. Retrieved August 31, 2022,
from https://bibleanswers.study/

Unsplash.com. (n.d.). *Unsplash*. Unsplash. Retrieved August
31, 2022, from https://unsplash.com/s/photos/trust-in-god

Vicky Matheny. (2022). [Jumping for Joy, Kneeling in
Prayer, Rocket Ship].

Made in the USA
Las Vegas, NV
04 January 2023

64833808R00046